Sharks

Anne Schreiber

NATIONAL
GEOGRAPHIC

Washington

To Ben, who taught me to love unlovable animals.
— A.S.

Published by the National Geographic Society, Washington, D.C. 20036. All rights reserved.
Reproduction in whole or in part without written permission of the publisher is strictly prohibited.

ISBN: 978-1-4263-1579-4

Cover: © Tim Davis/CORBIS; Title Page: © Jeffrey L. Rotman/Getty Images; 2-3: © Gary Bell/
Oceanwideimages.com; 4-5: © David Fleetham/Mira/drr.net; 6(inset), 18(bottom, right):
© Shutterstock; 6-7, 11, 32(top, left): © Mark Conlin/V&W/Image Quest Marine; 7(inset), 18(middle),
19(top), 32(bottom, left): © Bob Cranston/SeaPics.com; 8-9, 18(top), 18(bottom, left), 32(bottom, right):
© Doug Perrine/SeaPics.com; 10: © Niall Benvie/Nature Picture Library; 12-13, 22(bottom), 32(center,
both): © Masa Ushioda/SeaPics.com; 14-15: © Kike Calvo/V&W/Image Quest Marine; 16-17, 19(bottom),
32(top, right): © Jeff Rotman/SeaPics.com; 20-21: © David Doubilet/National Geographic Image
Collection; 22(top): © James D. Watt/SeaPics.com; 22-23 (ribbon illustration): © Photodisc/Getty
Images; 23 (both): © C&M Fallows/SeaPics.com; 24-25: © Espen Rekdal/SeaPics.com; 26-27:
© Gary Bell/SeaPics.com; 28: © Steve Robertson/ASP/Covered Images/Getty Images; 29:
© Noah Hamilton Photography; 30-31: © David D. Fleetham/SeaPics.com.

Printed in the United States of America
13/WOR/1

Table of Contents

CHOMP!

What is quick?
What is quiet?
What has five rows of teeth?
What glides through the water?
CHOMP!
It's a shark!

Sharks live in all of Earth's oceans.
They have been here for a long time.
Sharks were here before dinosaurs

OCEANIC WHITETIP SHARK

CARTILAGE: Cartilage is light, strong and rubbery. The tip of your nose is cartilage. Can you feel how soft it is?

Shark tail fins are larger on top. This helps them move through the water better.

HAMMERHEAD SHARK

A shark is a fish. But a shark is not like other fish. Sharks do not have bones. They have soft cartilage instead. Cartilage helps sharks twist and turn. Cartilage helps

If a shark loses a tooth, a new one moves forward to take its place.

Shark skin feels bumpy and rough. It's hard like sandpaper. It protects sharks

Shark Pups

Shark babies are called pups. Some pups grow inside their mothers. Other pups hatch from eggs.

LEMON SHARK

Lemon shark pups grow inside their mothers. The lemon shark mother goes to shallow water to give birth. The pups stay near the shallow water until they are grown.

These fish are called remoras. They hang around sharks and eat their leftovers.

LEMON SHARK PUP

9

MERMAID'S PURSE

Swell shark pups hatch from eggs. The mother sharks lay the eggs in hard cases. People call the case a mermaid's purse.

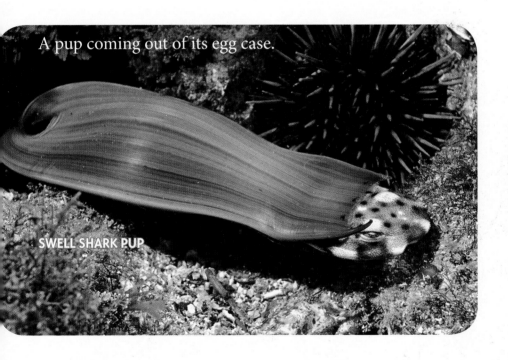

A pup coming out of its egg case.

SWELL SHARK PUP

Swell shark mothers lay up to five egg cases at a time. In nine months, the swell shark pups are born.

Pups Grow Up

NURSE SHARK

WORD BITES

PREDATORS: Animals that eat other animals.
PREY: Animals that are eaten by other animals.

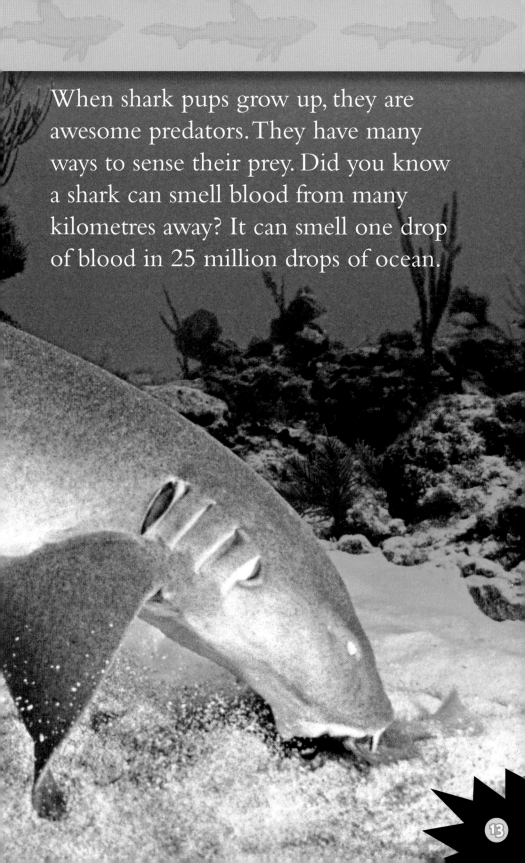

When shark pups grow up, they are awesome predators. They have many ways to sense their prey. Did you know a shark can smell blood from many kilometres away? It can smell one drop of blood in 25 million drops of ocean.

13

Sharks can see better than humans can. Even in deep, dark water, a shark can see its prey.

Sharks take a test bite of prey before eating. Their taste buds tell them if the prey is fat enough to eat.

GREAT WHITE SHARK

15

What Big TEETH You Have

SAND TIGER SHARK

Sharks have many rows of teeth.
They are always losing some teeth.
They are always growing new teeth.
A shark uses up more than 10,000
teeth in its life.

Different sharks have different teeth.
Their teeth are perfect for what they eat.

Long, spiky teeth are for catching.

Flat teeth are for grinding.

Serrated teeth are for ripping.

PREHISTORIC: Prehistoric is a time before people wrote things down.
EXTINCT: Extinct plants and animals are no longer alive on Earth.

MEGALODON TOOTH

Wow! Prehistoric sharks had really big teeth – up to 15cm! This made them fearsome predators.

The megalodon is a prehistoric shark. Scientists made a life-sized model of the megalodon's jaw and put in the teeth they have found. You can imagine how big the shark must have been.

Imagine This!

A giant shark is gliding through
the water.
A swimmer is nearby.
The shark gets closer.
It is huge.
It opens its giant mouth and…

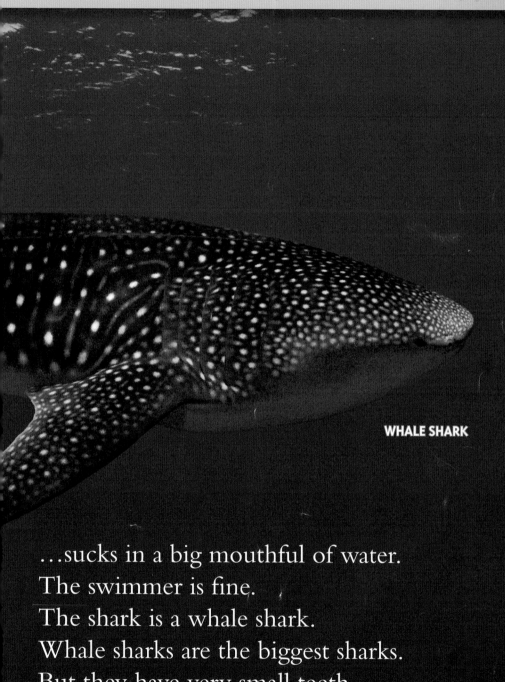

WHALE SHARK

…sucks in a big mouthful of water.
The swimmer is fine.
The shark is a whale shark.
Whale sharks are the biggest sharks.
But they have very small teeth.
They eat tiny animals called plankton.

Super Shark Awards

There are about 375 different types of sharks.

A hammerhead shark has a head shaped like a giant hammer. Its wide head is great for hunting.

WEIRDEST
The Hammerhead Shark

The spined pygmy shark is about 20cm long. It has a glow-in-the-dark belly.

SMALLEST
The Spined Pygmy Shark

CREEPIEST
The Great White Shark

When a great white bites its prey, its eyes roll back into its head. This protects its eyes.

FASTEST
The Mako Shark

The mako is the fastest shark. It can swim over 30km per hour. Makos leap clear out of the water to catch prey.

Now You See Them...

LANTERN SHARK

Some sharks glow in the dark! Do you see something shiny in the water? Watch out! The tiny lantern shark is covered with a glow-in-the-dark slime.

The lantern shark is a deep-sea shark. Many deep-sea animals glow. Scientists think glowing might help predators attract prey.

Most sharks are hard to see. They have a dark back. From above, they blend in with the water. They have a white belly. From below, they blend in with the sky.

WOBBEGONG SHARK.

Some sharks have special ways to hide. Wobbegongs have colours like the sea floor. Their mouths have parts that look like seaweed. Fish swim in but they can't get out!

Shark Attack!

One day Bethany Hamilton went surfing. Suddenly, a tiger shark attacked. It tugged her as she held onto her surfboard. It took a big bite out of her surfboard. It also took Bethany's left arm.

After the attack, Bethany wanted to keep surfing. She is not afraid to go in the water. She knows that shark attacks are rare.

Bethany says, "One thing hasn't changed – and that's how I feel when I'm riding a wave."

People Attack?

Shark attacks are scary and terrible. Sharks can be a danger to people. But people are a bigger danger to sharks. Millions of sharks die in nets set to catch other fish. Others are killed on purpose.

Many types of sharks may become extinct. Sharks have been on Earth for millions of years. Sharks and people need to learn to share the sea.

GREY REEF SHARK

CARTILAGE
Cartilage is light, strong and rubbery. Shark skeletons are made of cartilage.

EXTINCT
Extinct plants and animals are no longer alive on Earth.

PREDATOR
A predator is an animal that eats other animals.

PREY
Prey are animals that are eaten by other animals.

PREHISTORIC
Prehistoric is a time before people wrote things down.

SERRATED
When something is serrated, it has a jagged edge.